This Is a Let's-Read-and-Find-Out Science Book

CACTUS IN THE DESERT

By **Phyllis S. Busch**   Illustrated by **Harriett Barton**

T H O M A S   Y.   C R O W E L L   N E W   Y O R K

All plants need water. Some plants need a lot of
water. Others need very little.

Big trees in woods and forests need a lot of water. They grow where it rains many times in a year. A big tree in a forest may take in 800 quarts (about 760 liters) of water in a day. That's enough to fill two or three bathtubs all the way to the top.

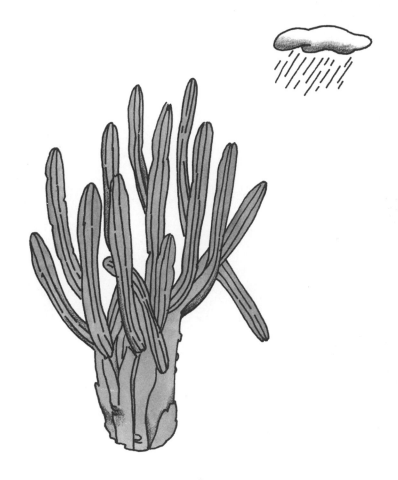

Plants that grow in hot, dry deserts—like cactus plants—need only a little water. Some of them grow where it rains only once or twice in a year.

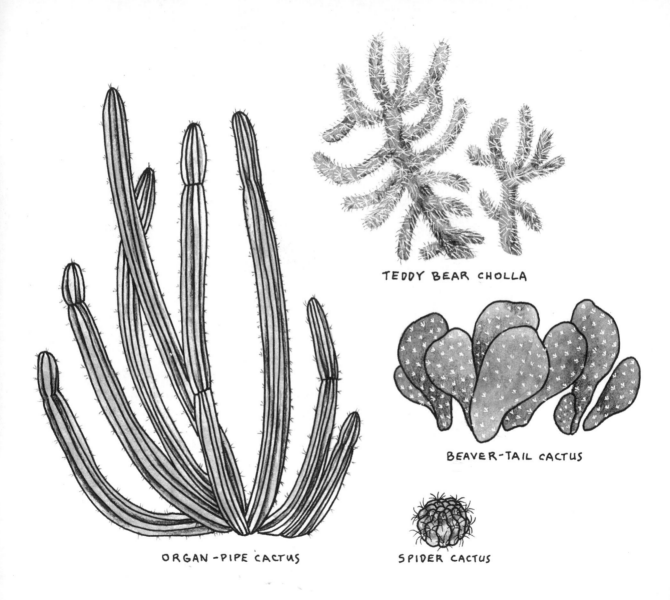

TEDDY BEAR CHOLLA

BEAVER-TAIL CACTUS

ORGAN-PIPE CACTUS

SPIDER CACTUS

6

Many different kinds of cactus plants live in
deserts. Some are very small. Others are very large.
The pincushion cactus is no bigger than your
thumbnail. Most cactus plants are bigger.

The tallest cactus is called the giant saguaro. It is also called a tree cactus. A saguaro has a big stem. It also has many branches that go straight up. It looks like a telephone pole with branches.

Some saguaros are almost 60 feet tall (about 18 meters). That's higher than ten people standing on each other's shoulders.

Big plants and little plants get water in the same way. So do plants in the forest and plants in the desert. They get water through their roots.

In leafy plants the water goes from the roots, up the stem, and into the leaves. The leaves use some of the water to make sugar and starch. These are foods for plants.

But most cactus plants have no leaves. They make sugar and starch in their stems.

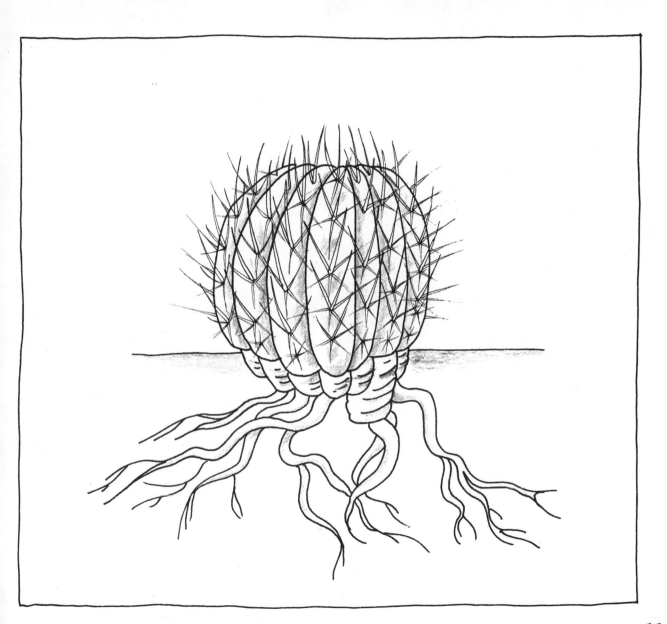

11

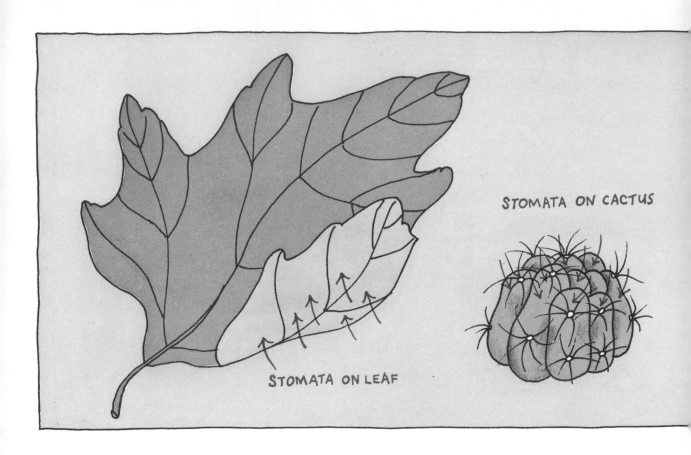

STOMATA ON CACTUS

STOMATA ON LEAF

Plants don't use all the water that they take in.
They give off nearly all of it. In most plants the
water goes out through small holes on the bottom
of the leaves. In a cactus the holes are in the stem.

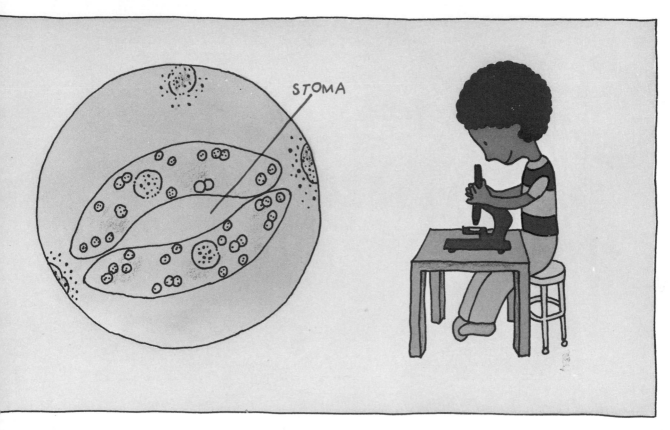

STOMA

A single hole is called a stoma. It's a word that means little mouth. Many holes together are called stomata. Whether they are in the leaves or in the stems, you need a microscope to see the stomata because they are so small.

When a plant is saving water, the stomata are closed. When it is giving off water, the stomata are open. The water evaporates. It goes into the air.

On a hot day an apple tree gives off a lot of water—as much as 320 quarts (about 300 liters) in a single day. Bigger trees give off even more.

A cactus plant also gives off water. But only a little bit. The stem has a very thick, tough skin. There are tiny stomata in the stem. But there are only a few of them, not nearly as many as there are in the leaves of leafy plants. Only a little water can evaporate into the air. On a hot day, a big saguaro cactus loses less than one glass of water.

Water is stored up inside a cactus plant. That is one reason why a cactus plant can live in the desert. It stores water for the long time when there is no rain. Cactus plants store water in their roots and their stems.

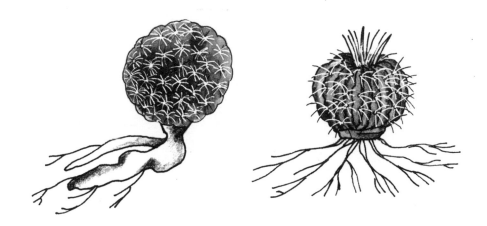

Some cactus plants have fat roots. Others have thin roots, but they have hundreds of them. And they spread out in all directions. The roots from a single plant might cover an area as big as a blanket. Sometimes the area is as big as a tennis court.

When it rains, these small roots collect the water from the whole area that they spread into. Both the fat roots and the thin roots take in a lot of water. The fat roots can store a lot of water, too.

Some cactus plants hold a lot of water in their stems. They look like watermelons covered with spines. The spines are as sharp as needles.

One kind is called a barrel cactus because it looks like a little fat barrel. When a cowboy in the desert needs water, he can get it by chewing a piece of this cactus. The watery juice inside is bitter, but the water will keep him alive. That's why people also call this cactus the traveler's friend.

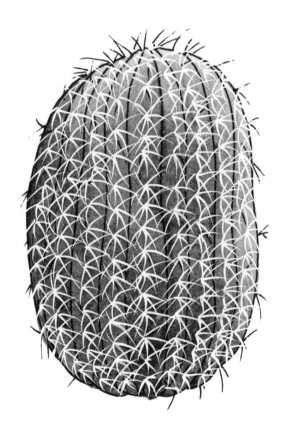

As the barrel cactus uses water, the stem shrivels up a bit.

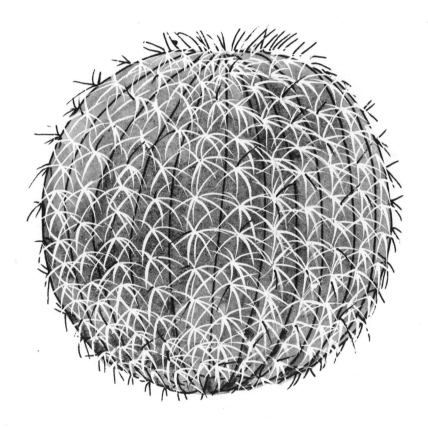

When it rains, the spiny stem fills up again.

Most cactus plants have spines on their stems. Some spines are short, straight, and hard. Other spines are longer, and are curved.

Indians used to break off the curved spines and
use them as fishhooks.

The sharp spines make it hard for most animals
to eat cactus plants. But wood rats eat them.

Cattle will eat cactus, too, if the cattle are
hungry enough.

Gila woodpeckers dig holes in cactus plants.
Then they make their nests in the holes.

When a cactus is cut, or when a bird digs a hole
in it, juice oozes out. But not for long. The juice
hardens over the cut, and so stops running out.
That's another way that cactus plants save water.

ladyfingers

bunny-ears

peanut

pincushion

Cactus plants grow well when they are in a hot dry place. You can find out for yourself. Maybe someone you know raises cactus plants and will give you one. Or you might buy one. These are some kinds you might get: bunny-ears cactus, ladyfingers cactus, peanut cactus, and pincushion cactus.

Indoors a cactus does best in a warm and sunny place. It needs only a little water.

It may grow so slowly that at times you will think it is not growing at all. Yet it may live in your house for years and years. There are cactus plants in the desert that are over 200 years old.